THE BOSNIA ELEGIES

THE
BOSNIA
ELEGIES

POEMS BY

ADRIAN OKTENBERG

PARIS PRESS

Ashfield, Massachusetts

1997

Acknowledgments

Grateful acknowledgment is made to the editors of journals in which some of the poems originally
appeared, sometimes in slightly different form: *The American Voice* and *Malachite and Agate*.

I am deeply grateful to the Astraea Foundation for its Astraea Lesbian Writers Fund Award, espe-
cially to Joan Drury, Katherine Acey, Olga Broumas and Kitty Tsui. This generous assistance came at
a crucial time. I am also very grateful for a grant from the Money for Women/Barbara Deming
Memorial Fund, Inc., given in support of this book.

I am indebted to Ruth Stone and Jan Freeman whose encouragement and belief in my work have
made it possible for me to go on writing. I regret that Henry A. Sauerwein, Jr. did not live to see this
book. His loyal friendship and support of my work over a number of years helped me immeasurably.
I will continue to miss him.

The main body of this book was written between June and December 1995. The Dayton peace
accords were signed in December 1995.

Paris Press acknowledges with gratitude the assistance of those who support its work. Publication of
this book is made possible in part by grants from individuals and Gilliland Printing, Inc.

This book is a work of art, not history or reportage. Although it refers to actual persons, places and
events, descriptions of these have sometimes been combined or altered in other ways. Statements
herein, therefore, are not necessarily to be taken as literally true.

This book was designed in Adobe Garamond type by Tree Swenson.
Author photograph by Jan Freeman.
UNHCR photograph on cover by A. Hollmann, reprinted by permission.
Epigraph from Charlotte Delbo, *Auschwitz and After*, tr. Lamont (New Haven and London: Yale
University Press, 1995). Copyright © 1995 by Yale University; reprinted by permission.

Library of Congress Cataloging-in-Publication Data
Oktenberg, Adrian, 1947-
The Bosnia elegies : poems / by Adrian Oktenberg — 1st ed.
p. cm.
ISBN 0-9638183-5-X (alk. paper)
1. Yugoslav War. 1991 - —Poetry. 2. Bosnia and Hercegovina-
—Poetry. I. Title
PS3565.K75B67 1997
811'.54—dc20 96-25030

Paris Press, Inc., P.O. Box 487, Ashfield, MA 01330

CONTENTS

This book is for the poets whose words and example made it possible:

Eavan Boland, Constantine Cavafy, Tory Dent, Carolyn Forché, Adrienne Rich, Ruth Stone, Walt Whitman

— and Jan Freeman

and for the people of Bosnia-Herzegovina, Croatia, and Serbia in solidarity

The weather was beautiful on that autumn day.
Beautiful for whom?

— *Charlotte Delbo, at Ravensbrück*

EARLY summer   newly formed leaves
like a baby's fingernails   no larger than a matchhead
Clouds gather   toward sunset
translucent veils
and the sky is like a bed
    a bed made up
    with a bedspread of eggshell blue
a bed in a white stucco farmhouse   red-tiled roof
    on a mountain turning pink
a mountain in another country
    the kind of country
    where a wooden hayfork
    still leans against a wall
Summer approaches
with promise   as this child's life is all possibility
They say a bloodred sunset
promises a gorgeous day

A HUNTER   A rabbit
   A swallow crossing the air
The way a land looks before disaster
something we never knew   or knew and have forgotten
and though the thousands   killed in a single morning at Antietam
still lie   they lie mute   we can't hear them
We rise and stand at the window   coffee in hand
watch birds crowd the feeder
remark on the lovely weather
Though we slap open a newspaper
we also spread jam on a piece of toast
thinking only a minute later
of work waiting at the office
You'll be home for dinner?

IN 1991, when Yugoslavia broke up   and ceased to exist."
    Croatia   Bosnia and Herzegovina   Serbia   Montenegro
    Slovenia   Macedonia
Now the Croats have retaken the Krajina
and 200,000 Serbs have taken to the roads   today
the announcement came   arrogant   intoxicated
        "The Krajina   has ceased to exist."
In 1991   when the Serbs   took the eastern third   of Croatia
and called it the "Krajina"   "Border-land"   the town of Vukovar
ceased to exist   wiped off the map
State of nature   war of   all against all
warring factions and bands   crisscross the land
        populations   dispersed   cleansed   disappeared
The death of nations formed in slaughter   conquest
murderous intent   We were always an ambiguous nation
        disloyal to nationhood   yet we continue to exist
We still struggle here below   broken   fallen down
        we are here   on this land
without roof or shelter
living like the animals now

THEY took the men of military age   marched them out
as if they were an army but they were not an army   they were men
fathers   brothers   brothers-in-law   uncles   nephews   sons
matchless with tools   song   supper   courtship
generous   handsome   proud   bearded   sunburnt   dressed
in the free clothes of workers   farmers   Sunday hunters   young men

They were brought out in squads and massacred   it was beautiful
                                                    full summer
the work commenced at five o'clock and was over by ten
Nobody obeyed the command to kneel
some made a rush   some stood stark and straight
a few fell at once   living and dead   lay mingled together
the maimed and mangled dug in the dirt   the newcomers saw them
some half-dead attempted to crawl away   were caught
and dispatched with a single bullet to the back of the neck
A youth not yet twenty-three seized his killer   until two more came
                                                     to release him
the three all torn and covered with the young man's blood

That day at Srebenica
that was a jetblack dawn

12

WHEN my mother was killed   I bitterly missed
her binding force   All Bosnia in pain
is only a little war   they say   bands against ragtag bands
The larger one   the one they speak of   with dread
when the mighty armies   of Croatia   and Serbia
fall against each other   with force
the "war in the Balkans"   the catastrophic ordeal
The Bosnian raped, maimed, dead   a brief shower of raindrops
thrown against the screen   in advance of the storm

MESSAGES

Messages sent all around the world   whispered
        from ear to ear   memorized   smuggled out
messages of danger   of catastrophe
rape   murder   torture   ethnic cleansing   camps
from Rwanda   Somalia   Kurdistan   China
        from Bosnia and Herzegovina
These are today's messages   tomorrow there will be more

Messages sent daily   Who sends them?   to whose ears?
These things matter
People are tuned to hear the messages
        of loved ones   countrymen   allied governments
        co-religionists   clan   all others discarded
Messages sent   sometimes they are heard
        or misheard   changed   twisted to others' ends   ignored
The message of a Black to a white one is heard differently
The message of a Jew or Muslim to a Christian ear
The message that travels from East to West is an utterly different message
        from one that falls solely among Western ears
Yet the messages are sent   they come in   come in on the news
        the airwaves   the fax

Messages   desperate messages of all kinds   too many messages
Who can begin to sort them?   to answer?
Still they send them   still they try
        human being to human being (that is their hope)
        seeking human help
In these times
the central message is of dying and not dying   at others' hands
the central message is of dying and not dying

IN the refugee camp
   she starts a diary in a tiny notebook   given to her by a worker
She writes only to remember she is alive   She owns a pen
She owns a pen

The entries are terse   the longest entry is eleven lines
Her brother's throat was slit before her
Her sister-in-law was raped and killed before her
She was raped many times
Her husband is gone
bussed away with the others
On the way out of the village, she saw bodies
hanging from trees

She wonders why she is here
Why is she still alive?

THE thousands who disappeared
after the fall of Srebenica
the few who fled through the mountains   in small groups   alone
two-by-two
wounded   exhausted   pursued
afraid to encounter another on the path
the earth shook behind them   torched barns and houses   their thirst
This   mountainous country   rough terrain   unyielding
to human frailty   folly   need
Three or four thousand made their way through the Serbian lines
the UN reported   in the next few days
What of the others?   What is the fate of the others?

IN the morning
 after the fall of Srebenica and Zepa
they found the body of the young woman
in the refugee camp   hanging from a tree
It was high summer   It seemed she had turned to leaves overnight
and how lightly she flew   She was weightless now
She had become   a spoil of war
They said she was raped at Srebenica
raped by the Serbs at Srebenica
on a floodlit bed   Her rapes filmed
        shown on television   in Banja Luka
        the voice-over said she was Serb
They said she felt herself   spoiled by war
She had gone mad they said
They carried her body through the camp on a stretcher
Everyone saw
Everyone saw

LIKE an American movie star of the Fifties
    thick   black   wavy hair
someone like Victor Mature
Dr. Radovan Karadzic   chief of the Pale Serbs
before the war a psychiatrist   a convicted embezzler
he served eleven months in Sarajevo jail
        plays and picks

Sixty thousand rapes?
Women raped many times?   He smiles at the reporter
A distinct impossibility!   He explains the facts of life
That would mean thirty thousand children
At least thirty thousand children

                        (He knows the exact degree
                        of virility of his men.
                        Their sperm is like his own.)

He frowns   Where are all these children?
Why can't they be found?
He shifts   and his head his smile   look
        remarkably like Papa Stalin's
Give them to me!   he declares
I will adopt them all!

THE systematic destruction   of a people
        by government policy   acted out   on a deliberate scale
not scattered atrocities   however unfortunate   committed
        in the heat of war
The UN delegate   defines   genocide   on television
She wears   a diplomat's dress   navy blue   a tasteful pin
Her deeply lined faced   troubled   she speaks
        a modulated voice   It is
an evening   deep in summer   and I have gone outside
for just a minute   in the gathering dusk   to pick my first tomato
the one I have been watching   for weeks, very closely   in the last few days
It is a question of gathering   she says   the evidence
from various sources   to find how high up
in the government   the policy starts   who is responsible
It is a long process   growing a tomato   which starts
late in spring   when the earth is beginning to warm   and now the flesh
I bring it   in and gently wash and dry it and put it on the desk
        an unlikely place   for a tomato   isn't it?
Doesn't it long for a salad?
The flesh is the color of   meat   like a raw steak, mottled
bruised with green   near the stem   The delegate
talks about the process   The satellite photos
show the mass graves   The soccer field
where people had been crowded   only days before   now empty
The farmer's fields with fresh-turned earth   and the tracks
there are always tracks, somewhere   if you know how and where to look
of heavy equipment   You need heavy equipment   she says
to bury   that many people   and it leaves scars on the earth
You can see them   in the photograph   here, and here
She points with a small baton
We think 1,200 souls   maybe more   too early to say
the process   I pick it up in both hands   my tomato   press it
against my lips   it smells of earth   of the long days of sun
and earth

19

OUT of the shards of the ruined house
an old woman collects belongings
In her bundle   a photograph   a book
partially burned   there is a cooking pot
She gathers them   bending
A strange silence hovers   like smoke over the scene
No one is there to help   No one is in the distance
Where will she go, alone?   What will she cook in her pot tonight?
Will she sleep in a ditch at the edge of a field?
Who will help her?   Who knows?

WHY do men   confuse   their own ambition
     with history?   Mladic the old party man   and Karadzic
are men like that   they claim   Serbia is everywhere
Serbs are   even in Vienna   where they have fled by the thousands
their leaders' war   Remember: this is not a war of conquest
they say   The dream of Greater Serbia   is an old one
          folk songs   stories of heroes   centuries past
They will use   any means   to achieve their aims
Hitler too   claimed to rescue   the Sudetenland Germans
     from harassment   and atrocity
The claims for war   are always   old and good ones
     our traditions   our way of life   our history
Atrocities made   in our names   are always claimed
     as justice   redress

THE drought   causes the chestnut leaves   to curl
    with brown along the edges   and acid rain
makes all the apples fall   in August   littering the ground
You have to know how   and where   to look for disaster
in this country   It is not   like crossing a field
        not the artillery shell   falling in a school yard
        the child   his face star-crossed with shrapnel   still clutching
a toy   On the eastern rim   of the horizon   where blue
melts into summer white   Is that where it begins?
Fields   dark green   thick with corn
fields   bright green   planted with sweet alfalfa
Dry rutted roads   where farmers' tractors pass
from time to time   brilliant in the light

THE Serbs won't let the Red Cross in
to see the camps
The UN High Commissioner   the rescue committee
all are concerned   They issue a protest   in the strongest terms
All reported   written
papers strewn across the whole body   of the countryside
pictures disseminated   the whole world knows
They negotiate   talk   send new representatives
Now the Swedish representative comes
Days pass   weeks   months
Mladic and Karadzic   indicted at the tribunal   in The Hague
Who will arrest them?   When will they be brought to court?
        the indictments   make negotiation   difficult
the situation   complicated   Days pass   months
And this   (Charlotte tells us)   is what a day in the camps is like
every minute   an exhaustion   blind with suffering:
surviving a single day   is like surviving hell in eternity
It is not like crossing   an open field
They continue to talk   days   months pass
the camps continue to exist

IT was an open-air market   in full swing   midday February 1994
The stalls were nearly bare   a few cabbages   garlic
UN lunch packets   humanitarian aid   macaroni and rice
Old clothes   small sizes only   utensils
plastic for blasted windows   very rare and dear
Nevertheless it was crowded   deutsche marks only accepted
noisy with bargaining   The city under siege   for some time
People learned to take some risks
Besides, they had to live   When the shell screamed in
limbs, a severed head, flew   bodies   broken equipment
     bloody tissue   sirens
Rescue workers ran   calling to each other
working fast   Sixty-eight were killed   in a moment
many wounded   The UN called a conference   The "contact group"
                                                            of five
met five times   This was after   the shelling of the bakery line
the shelling of the water line   and Sniper Alley
A "pin-prick" air-strike   was called
down on a single Serbian gun   in the mountains above the city
Now the main Sarajevo market   is in an alley six feet wide

THERE was a woman in Bihac
when Bihac was under siege
and about to fall

There was a woman in Bihac
who sent a short-wave message
and the message said
"Is there no one left in the world to help us?"

The message
was reported on the evening news
The message
was not answered
The message of the woman in Bihac
became a ghost-message

TOWNS we believe and die in"   Srebenica   Zepa   Bihac
"protected" by UN troops   Bihac under siege   three years
children died of starvation   Croatian troops
lifted the siege   routed the Bosnian Serbs   betrayed
by their patron Milosevic   and the UN protected nothing
neither Serbs nor Muslims   The Muslims   even while they celebrate
in the streets   don't trust the Croatians their saviors
The Bosnian Serbs   are bitter toward their mother Serbia
even while they flee   for miles crowd the roads   toward her arms
The ironies of this war   layer on layer   will change again

THE young Muslim said to his uncle   My heart
beats now with a single hope
The Croatians, Uncle   the Croatians
are back in the fight   Let them win
and I will give anyone who fought
my farm   my horses   my mother's red coral . . .

The uncle may have been moved   a little
but then he remembered   his brother, his two sons
He said nothing

IN Sarajevo   there lived a girl
Zlata Filipovic´ was her name   who began to keep a diary
in which   she counted up her losses   longings
Zlata wanted   to go to the movies   the disco   to school
to sit in a café   with her friends
She wanted her grandmother back   their farm
but the siege   kept her   inside the apartment
kept her   in cellars   Until the French reporter   found out
put her on television   made her read the diary
into the cameras   filmed her   looking out a blasted window
        the American media   made a splash
Her sadness   framed the pictures   They talked about Anne Frank
that diary and doom the Jewish people
and the new Anne Frank   of Sarajevo   The rescuers
        bore her up   above the city
flew her   away from the war her past her people
and behind her   Sarajevo   still under siege

WHO dares to speak of Beauty   in this war?   Who
dares to speak   at all?
The aged poet   sits in her apartment   in Sarajevo
and the reporter   delicately asks   about the intellectuals
The intellectuals   she says   the ones who left   the ones
who now pursue   café philosophy   in Paris   or Prague
Let them keep silent
They have nothing to say
to us   who stayed

OUR room   how well I know it
   though now   the outside wall is gone   the floor
what's left   sags   like a bird's nest   open to the sky
But I see the sink   still clings to its wall
This other destruction   came later   only a destruction of things

Here   near the door   was the couch   old
from the Twenties   stuffed with horsehair   and its gracious curve
a carpet   its pattern of delicate shell-pink and brown

Here   the shelf   with my two vases   I used to love
to bring you roses   white ones, or Champagne   never red
On the right—no, opposite   your wardrobe
with a mirror   I used to watch you   slowly brush your hair
In front of the window   the tiny table where I wrote
Beside the window the bed
where we made love so many times   and you used to bring me coffee

Beside the window the bed   the afternoon sun
used to touch just half of it
One afternoon   we separated   only briefly
and forever came so swiftly I —

IN August 1914
"somewhere in the Balkans"   a shot was fired
        and in the summer of 1936   a coup took place
and each time   *each* time
        a war was fought in Europe
        and Europe was destroyed

"The first century of world wars"
        is our century   coming to its awful end

and this is the dangerous summer
        at the end of the century

in which we know these things
in which we were supposed to know these things

THOSE who are forced to live in this city
        the airport closed   the highways sealed
the Serbs hurling shells down   from the mountains around us
live like rats   in basements and tunnels
The UN brings in food and water   only by permission of the Serbs
The UN envoy   humiliated   not allowed to use the airport,
                                        has to leave by truck .

We starve slowly
Survival is automatic   mechanical   an exercise in futility
How to get water   food   a little heat
We grow vegetable patches   on every former strip of grass
tended in the brief moments   when one can go outside
Ratushinskaya ate a salad of goosefoot   pronounced the taste
                                        wonderful:
we read that once   in a book   in our former life
But we don't think of our former life   that is the dangerous path
the Sarajevo Olympics   1984   when the world came and loved us
Torvill and Dean were flawless   a perfect score   thrilling
The mountains were for skiers   so beautiful   ringing the city
now we look at them with dread
the past   too dangerous   memory   the surest route to madness
We who used to look   on the city of Beirut   with pity
We are a former people   in a former city   in "the former Yugoslavia"
Wood is unheard-of, all used up   unimaginable luxury
We burn shoe leather   former schoolbooks   anything that lasts
        scavenge on piles of rubble   for usable scrap
The *Collected Lenin* is an ideal gift for a lover   Lenin burns very well
Trolleys no longer run   too much a provocation
passengers picked off by snipers   one by one
To cross the city by foot   to find a usable tap   a UN water-truck
                                        a basement
is to take one's life in one's hands   you have to be able to run
        fast across the open spaces   in the sniper's hairs

a sport for young men only   but old women also are forced to play
the hellish tunnel   dank   black   with shelling at both ends
the return trip is always worse: water is heavy, like the dead weight
of a body dragged behind you
The city has only a six-week supply of flour   the last bakery may close
Without bread, what then?   There are mothers
who eye their babies speculatively   Without antibiotics,
surgical dressings, anesthetics, the wounded pile up   in the wards
hospitals turn to charnel houses   a shot to the head is to be preferred
In Sarajevo   we tell the former tourists   we have two ways to die
                                               fast, or slow

ONE afternoon   we separated   only briefly
     you went to the market   It was the end of August
a Monday   the first sunny day   after days
of rain   The main Sarajevo market   was indoors then
a sixteenth century building   thick walls of stone
but there was a crowd   at the entrance   a policeman
had tried to disperse it   minutes before   two shells came in
together   thirty-seven killed   a hundred wounded   in an instant
     a man's body impaled   on the fence   an old man
dead on the ground   his legs still wrapped   around his motorcycle
bodies fell to pieces as they were lifted   into cabs
A woman ran up the steps at the hospital   her child limp in her arms
     her face   you don't want to look at her face
A doctor shouted as he ran   "The world doesn't care
about us!"   The Kosevo hospital   the best in the world
after three years   of siege   and here   overflowing despair
battle-hardened nurses   wail and wave their arms
     and I went there but you had been in that crowd
They posted a list   I read your name
So after a while I went back to our room   not knowing what else to do
where else to go

THERE was no inevitability   to this war
        (though Americans love to think so)
There might have been no war
        things might have been different   if Bush   for instance
and his Texan Secretary of State—now *that's* a farce   had not decided
        we were a European problem   to be solved by Europeans only
        You can only tell this story as satire
Now, with peace talks   this partition   comes three years late
we could have had the same division   three years ago
        How many have died?   Over 11,000   in Sarajevo
        Two hundred thousand   in the war   thousands more
        maimed   450,000 refugees this summer alone
The beginning   middle   end   a continual unraveling
        almost as complex   in these borderlands
as the beginning   middle   end   of the universe
        and where in that time   on that time scale   are we now?
Can you tell me exactly?   I didn't think so

Turkish coffee
legacy of the time   when Constantinople ruled these lands
        The Serbs   call the Muslims   "Turks"
This story   has no closure   and will go on   if not in Bosnia
then in Kenya   Rwanda   Algeria   Sri Lanka   China   Brazil
and unravel again   the form for it is a spiral   an ancient form
        a spiral   of memory
Memory persists   with or without speech
Spoiled memory   humiliated memory   memory broken
        into its heartbroken parts   every strand shredded
Common memory   deep memory
ruined by this war

If I were you   since you have asked me
        since you wish to report   knowing you still have a duty

35

to report   I would suggest you look   at the broken-down places
      not walls and windows   though that is a start
Examine the remnants   of what was once our life
      our communal life   our common life

A YOUNG sniper   A single sparrow
A sparrow crosses the air
        in Sniper Alley   His eye
is briefly on the sparrow   magnified   in his lens
        He enjoys a pretty sight
He can see   anyone who moves   into the open
in search of food or water   or in search of a hasty death
as easily as if he were watching a film
        a thriller in which he is the shooter the hero the man with the gun
        his finger rests lightly on the trigger   ready to squeeze
        his own personal film and he can   shoot any one he likes
He is calm and happy   at ease   the city is at his feet
He knows he is free
His eye is on the sparrow   and I am here below
I know he is watching me   I live
a few blocks from Sniper Alley and I go   in order to live
        across the open space   there is no way to judge
the degree of safety or danger   in this topsy-turvy world
        you must go   this choice too has been taken from you
        by this war
the whole of the Balkans is but a mote   in God's glass eye
        a single slap   there is no noise   she doesn't hear a noise
sprawled on the pavement, skirt splayed above her waist, blood
        comes from somewhere, she doesn't know where
She has a daughter she thinks of her daughter she is unable to move

He knows he is free
His eye is on the sparrow
and I know he is watching me

37

LIKE everything else   our language   is particular to us
    Outsiders cannot learn it   it's gibberish to them
Yesterday   I heard a woman say   "This war has destroyed my life"
Why do we always say   "this war"?
To acknowledge   the wars that came before?
To remember   future wars?
To say   *this* war   is to acknowledge   *that* one
          the last one   and the one yet to come
When we say   "this war"   we already envision another
But *which* war   is the last war?   Will there ever be one?
That woman who spoke   she was a Serb   caught outside Banja Luka
     in a Croatian   artillery barrage   her ten-year-old killed
     she and her nineteen-year-old   seriously wounded
Severed arteries in her leg and arm   If she recovers
     what will she recover for?   This war
     begets another and another
     an old testament book
The new testament
love and charity and forgiveness   the lilies of the field
                    that one hasn't been written

AFTER the offensive   the morgue is filled
a makeshift morgue in a still-standing house with a sagging porch
on the porch   bodies are piled   like cordwood
bodies dressed in civilian clothes   two
with their eyes gouged out   one
          a seventy-two-year-old woman
There are a million ways to lose in a war
The Serbs were victorious proud   against weaker forces
          against women and children   but now they have spent
three years drinking   Arkan of the Tigers
          sounds like a football team but he's a warlord   says
          after three years of drinking
          they couldn't win against an army of Scouts
The Croatians slaughter   with equal abandon
          this war   will not turn tail and rout
This war is all   a revenge of memory
          and the winter snows
          will soon come
          obliterating nothing

THESE crazy countries   no one can keep them straight
        the confusion is endless   and the people
have unpronounceable names   no one has ever heard   of these towns
        it's too hard to care   another war
in some little country   somewhere   and their factions and bands
        I'm sure they're corrupt   look at this warlord
Arkan   formerly a sweetshop owner   now with his band the Tigers
        a huge knife and gun on his hip   really!
        his special dealings in who-dares-to-know   that kind of stuff
        his patron Milosevic   a dove
after doing his best to start the war   the economy in shambles
        whole industries stopped   for lack of parts
        guilty of war crimes   ethnic cleansing   mass rape
Milosevic talks peace   a diplomat says   only to hold on to power
        he doesn't care   he'll let the enemy occupy anything
right up to the block where he lives   he won't send the Yugoslav Army in
        now to save the Bosnian Serbs   they can all be slaughtered
He would rather not have them   he says   in Serbia
        if they should cease to exist   they would cease to trouble him
Milosevic talks peace to stay in power
        and the Croats make battlefield gains
they think they should be senior partners   very senior
        in the so-called "Federation"   with the Bosnian Muslims
        collect more territory   in the deliberations
        they argue they have earned it   on the ground
These internecine battles   have gone on in this region
        for centuries   and it's not Kuwait they have no oil
anyway it's too complicated   and hard to care
You can't even pronounce their names

DARLING, your face is turning white
becoming featureless   an untracked field of snow
Your eyes which once burned   like blue sky
        are flattening out   memory fails us both
I curse my failing memory   try to catch it
        it disappears around a bend   another   another
The exact timbre of your voice   the gesture
that moved me so   the way your laughter began
        deep in your chest   in your chest
        three pieces of shrapnel   were buried
three years ago

EXILE from home   this unwilled voyage
          yesterday she was still at her job   a secretary   today a refugee
These small countries   Colin Powell said the other day
          a mistake to recognize them
they ebb and flow   high tides and low   of refugees
                    farm wagons
drawn by horses   horses beaten, killed   tractors   gasless cars
          with nowhere to go
At the gates of the city   officials direct them
          to a town forty miles south
          back on the road on which they had come
hungry, thirsty, poor   it took their last strength to reach the city
          they are forced back
retrace their route   forty miles south
          to another town
          where there is no one to receive them
          no food or shelter
          they eat rumors and exhaustion now

BANJA LUKA you see was always a Serbian city
and so presents no problem but Sarajevo
the jewel the Jerusalem of these lands the center, the symbol
the that-which belongs to everyone
and so everyone wants it
at least a piece
They will leave it off the table
too difficult
too polyglot
and that is the trouble with this peace so-called plan
it rewards ethnic cleansing
ratifies it
purifies the land crystallizes borders
where no borders divided us before
This land is Croat, that for the Serbs
the Bosnian Muslims will have their own unequal piece
so-called peacekeeping troops will separate the groups
wall them off from each other
to keep them from fighting once again
Before the war Yugoslavia was not like that
and Sarajevo is still its symbol
a terrible mixture
You cannot divide each neighborhood suburb street house
family

THE Bosnian Serbs are farmers
    how they love to plant and till
their energy   has no bounds
In Srebenica   there was a stadium
packed with a thousand men   no games today
not the usual kind   now the stadium is empty
and the field nearby   is filled
with fresh-turned earth

THE West promises much   if only Bosnia will agree
      half a billion dollars
      if they will talk and stop the war
The Bosnians at last are winning   gaining ground fast
      so they are not so sure   they want to stop
they send out   an appeal   to Bosnians everywhere   Prague
      Budapest   Italy   New York
"Come back and fight!   The liberation of your homeland
is at hand!   You will be ashamed   when you come back
      if the job was done   by someone else!"

IN Sarajevo   I was happy there
   cafés   theater   nightlife   twenty minutes to the mountains
      three hours to the sea
a good job   a cosmopolitan life
      but when the war started   I felt unsafe
so I came to Belgrade   to live among my own
I thought   a better life   no shelling here
      there is water   electricity that works
      neighbors are not suspicious   except in the usual ways
but Belgrade is flat   flat   neither mountains nor sea
      life is flat   cut off from friends
      you cannot even telephone   Sarajevo   from here
      the train no longer runs
and the people   brother and sister Serbs
treat us like strangers
as if we are riffraff   scum

MY mother's death   lacked dignity
She who had bound us all together
like a tightly wound spool of twine   never a loose strand
left unbound for long   she who watched over it
vigilant   for any stray defection   and reached
to bring it back   she who would not *let* any one of us go away
She was left   cut off   like so many loose ends of twine
discarded on the floor of a busy workroom   while work
went on   above her   around her   And she   wounded
unable to speak   alone
while others talked and slept   in the crowded room
The apartment house   still stands
a shell   her body shoveled somewhere
under the rubble

IF I could find sleep   if I could dream
      I would dream of you   as you were   in the café
We drank brandy   Turkish coffee   talked
      into the night   our friends   talking politics   or books
      there are no books left
      all burned   their pages ash
The planes of your face   the way you talked
      when you were thrilled   by an idea
      and the animating spirit   that lighted your face

I sometimes take out your passport to stare at your picture

I T'S very much like him   this little pencil portrait
    it's a wonder I still have it   found
   in this old wooden box with the broken lid
   I wonder   what impelled me   to open it
           try as I might I can't get it closed

Quickly sketched   on the sloop's deck
   the afternoon magical
   nearly naked, in the sun
   the Adriatic sparkling around us

It is like him   not bad   but I remember him as stronger
   around the chin
   the way he held his mouth
   made him look perpetually amused

Now that time out of exit brings him back

Out of time   All this was very long ago
   the sketch   the sloop   the afternoon

NO no no   you don't understand   Just imagine
    for one moment   what it would take   to make you flee
your home forever   A polite knock   from an official stranger?
No it is not like that   First there are three years   of living like a bum
in your own town   the lost jobs   threats   harassments
beatings in the streets   the struggle to live   hated by your neighbors
the former friends who turned away and spat
One night   a note appears on the door: "This is a Serb house"
                                or   "This — Croatian"
The next morning   police come and seize the keys
Then   before you have time to think   soldiers come
                rifles   rifle butts   buses
People are crowded around   lots of people   armed
they are shouting   cursing   kicking in the door   smashing windows
You have seen   the ones who tried to resist   throats slashed
No   nothing else but terror   makes you gather up and leave
drawers left open   clothes on the floor
food still warm on the plates   the bicycle leaning
against the tree in the yard—it will be stolen
as anything of use or value is stolen   down to the bathroom tiles
You are in the yard   then in the street   and they are shouting
threatening and   crowding you all onto buses
but you can't leave   though now you are dying to leave
anything to get away quickly   They demand money
so much per head to board the bus   you know you *must* board this bus
but you don't have the fee   or only a little   or you and your family
will die here and now   The street is a chaos   of shouting and guns
shots into the crowd   a few fall bleeding   cries
Those who have money   hasten to pay it   others borrow
beseech their neighbors   but this once
by some miracle   those who have money give it   and only when
everyone's money has been given up   do you board the bus stumbling
You go   You don't know where you are going   You go
That is called ethnic cleansing   that is how it works

LET me tell you the story of my friend   the actress
          and you will see   what hatred has done to art
          what happens   when art is on the run
At the height of her fame and power   thirty-six years   strong
          appears regularly in the theater   in Zagreb   Medea, Blanche duBois
          the glossy covers of magazines   television   film
It happens she is Croat   it happens her husband is Serb
          but that is not unusual
          every year she went to Belgrade   to perform
          even during this war   but that was not unusual
          this year she made a public statement   that was her crime
She said she could not accept   ethnic categories
          classifications   inimical to art
          she would remain   as she had always been   an artist
          without category   an artist   devoted to her art
          art has no politics   she said   it is for all
          it has no ethnicity   she would accept no designation
          she would be neither one nor the other   but one for all
          all the newspapers printed   the actress's words
When she returned to Zagreb   the letters and telephone calls started
          graphic letters   calling her   all kinds of names
          at all hours   the middle of the night
          the callers told her exactly   what they would do to her
          exactly how they would do it
          they called again
          the calls and letters did not stop
          her headaches and nightmares began and did not stop
She and her husband fled
          left without winter clothes   or even papers
          friends met them in Paris
In New York   she sits in a borrowed apartment
          perched on the arm of a couch   thin   smoking incessantly
They move to a different friend's apartment   every few days
There are no roles   in Serbo-Croatian   in New York

ALL that he'd hoped for   turned out wrong

He'd seen himself doing great things
ending the humiliation   that had kept his people down
ever since the Battle of the Field of Blackbirds   in 1389
He'd seen himself   making the Serbs   powerful
      with armies   industries   wealth
      a nation standing up   that has stood up   at last

He'd suffered in Belgrade   become bitter
      when he sensed in the talk of friends
      in spite of their politeness   their kindness toward him
      a certain distance
      there was always a secret contempt   for the Bosnian Serbs:
they were inept   unfit for anything serious   fatally unable
to unite and rule their people   they thought Karadzic was a joke
not a man like Milosevic   He grew sick of them all

He'd cut himself off   searing   indignant
swearing things would be quite different   from the way they thought
Why   wasn't he himself   full of determination?
He would act   he would fight   he would put things right

And now?
      The young men in Belgrade   were right
      Betrayed by Milosevic   the Bosnian Serbs   losing ground
      Perhaps they would end with   a partial state   ruled by Belgrade
                             enclosed by the Turks
      the dream of a Greater Serbia   close to dead

He began to convince himself   it didn't matter
He'd made the effort   fought as well as he could

If he is betrayed by his leaders   what is a good soldier to do?
          forced to fall back and back   on the battlefield
                release territory without a fight
          because his leaders have judged   it is better to lose land
               in nonexistent battle   than to explain to the people
          why it was given up at a table   agreed to on a map

He is tired   and in his disillusion
          there's one thing only that gives him pride
even in failure   he still shows the world courage
          trying to keep his small family together
               out on the roads
The war was a dream   his courage   his hopes   wasted
This Bosnia   no longer seems like his country
He has become   a refugee in his own homeland

AT a dinner   commemorating the end   of World War II
fifty years ago   Tudjman sat   a proud new head of state
and this was already an irony   of this war
Fifty years ago   the Croatian Ustashe   fought on the Nazi side
        exterminated   seven hundred thousand Serbs and Jews
Someone asked   What will Bosnia look like   ten years from now?
He picked up a menu   and on the back   drew a rough circle
        for Bosnia   drew a wavy line down the middle   noted
the Croats on one side   Serbs on the other
        dividing the country   roughly in half
It will look like this   he said   and put his pencil down
        His questioner did not ask him
where was the place for the Bosnian Muslims   where will the Muslims go
They were not there   on Tudjman's menu
missing   disappeared

THEY are finding mass graves   and in them
    "Ustashe"   "Chetnik"   "Turk"
            local terms of hate
                        haven't we heard it all before?
We can lip-sync all the words
the language changes details change but it's the same
        always the bloated bodies in the rivers
        always the fields of skulls
        always the absent criminals   unwilling to be found
the subject of half-hearted ineffectual investigations

Television wars and slaughters
it's only another war
        the crazy Balkans
        we are so tired   tired of hearing
What can anyone do?   It's bad, I know   but it's someone else's crisis
I still have my life
My father's sick again   I think my uncle might be gay
You never know   any more   what's in the water
        the electricity lines   the built-over toxic dump
Cancer may still   get me in the end
and I eat   too much fat

ARLY October   A hunter's moon rises
illuminating grasses   each blade and branch is distinct
wind sweeps the leaves   off the trees
unclaimed gold   wastes on the ground
When the bliss of fall passes   preparation for sleep
and winter brings   starvation rations
wrecks of houses   trucks   looted possessions
protruding from snow   freezing soldiers
civilians with nowhere to go   Will the hunter begin to find his gun
a burden   his killer's passion slaked   Will he feel
a need to rest   Will the chilling catcalls of the dead
remind him   to attend   his blighted soul
Will exhaustion   bring this land
a measure of peace?

AWAY   we fled houses   past suburbs   outside the town
   Outside   Do you understand?
The town emitted   a high thin sound
the music of the concertina wire   a sound to burst the eardrums

Dense as a plow horse's mane   rain in our eyes
and mountains   huge in our eyes
    past suburbs   outside of the town   Do you understand?
A ditch   by the road   Two children are standing
a brother and sister pair   a field with an electric fence
    and this ditch   we cook a pot of rice in the rain
Ah   what a lost cause this is   ladies and gentlemen
They gave me a yellow paper   certificate of refugee status
I stamp it   with my feet
All Bosnia
is a towering mountain   standing in its own blood

WINTER snows
        how quiet   they make the whole world seem
Far back in the woods   a branch cracks with ice
        the sound of a pistol shot   to the back of the neck
And the large depressions   in the earth   where the snow
        a white blanket   like a comforter   seems to sag a little
All the little towns   around Banja Luka
        have depressions like that
        where April will show   bones   tatters of clothing   sticking out
After the peace descends   they will unearth the bodies
        like digging potatoes   for years to come
The survivors will remember the victims, the places, the names of the towns
        and tell their children   "Never forget!"
The Bosnian soldier   moving on Banja Luka said
"We fight for two things only
Freedom
and revenge"

NO one can tell you   how to live
no guides exist   when survival   is the only rule
This young man   today   only twenty-five
        one of only ten   survivors from his town
kneels on the muddy ground and gathers   the pieces of his father's
                        and grandfather's gravestones
He tries to   piece   together the names
"Can you read it?   Can you read it now?"   he keeps saying
"Can you see   what their names were?   Can you see them?"
Even his memory   is tainted   wounded   No one can tell him
how to live his life   once he has lived through this
he has gone beyond help
An hour's walk   in the quiet forest   as the afternoon sun deepens
the light in the top branches
Even so *and at the same time*   the world is so beautiful
Even so and at the same time   hold it in the mind

THE world is full of stoppable horrors   Who can count them?
Who would try?
The messages continue to come in   daily, hourly
    desperate messages   messages of all kinds
    the second-to-second pulses   of lives flickering out
The messages come in   come in   come in   come in   come in
and disappear